Lightning Bolt Books™



# Cool Kid Online Stars

Laura Hamilton Waxman

Lerner Publications ◆ Minneapolis

For Caleb, online fanatic and good kid —L.H.W.

Lerner Publications Company
An imprint of Lerner Publishing Group, Inc.
241 First Avenue North
Minneapolis, MN 55401 USA

For reading levels and more information, look up this title at www.lernerbooks.com.

**Library of Congress Cataloging-in-Publication Data**

Names: Waxman, Laura Hamilton, author.
Title: Cool kid online stars / Laura Hamilton Waxman.
Description: Minneapolis : Lerner Publications, [2020] | Series: Lightning bolt books—kids in charge! | Includes bibliographical references and index.
Identifiers: LCCN 2019020810 (print) | LCCN 2019022065 (ebook) | ISBN 9781541577022 (lb : alk. paper) | ISBN 9781541589148 (pb : alk. paper)
Subjects: LCSH: Online social networks—Juvenile literature. | Child celebrities—Juvenile literature.
Classification: LCC HM742 .W39 2020 (print) | LCC HM742 (ebook) | DDC 302.30285—dc23

LC record available at https://lccn.loc.gov/2019020810
LC ebook record available at https://lccn.loc.gov/2019022065

Manufactured in the United States of America
1-46724-47715-7/30/2019

# Table of Contents

# Bright Stars

Some kids are like the nighttime stars. They shine brightly. That's true for famous kids online. They catch a lot of attention.

These stars make popular videos on YouTube. They're funny, smart, clever, and creative. They have thousands or even millions of fans.

# Fun and Funny

Do you like to laugh? These online stars do. Their hilarious videos show off their fun and funny talents.

Evan and his family make slime in some of their videos.

## Evan

Evan started making videos with his family in 2011 on his channel, EvanTubeHD. They do silly challenges. They try wild experiments. They have millions of fans.

## Jillian and Addie McLaughlin

Sisters Jillian and Addie McLaughlin like to make people laugh. Their most popular channel is babyteeth4.

You can make people laugh by dressing up and acting out a silly story.

Talking about your favorite food or candy is an easy way to make a video.

The sisters became famous doing silly candy reviews. They also star in goofy skits and short movies. Their dad films all the fun.

# Kid Teachers

Some online stars like to share what they know. They get kids thinking and trying new things.

If you have a special skill or talent, you can make a video teaching it to others.

## Mya Reyes

Mya Reyes wanted to share her love of science. She began showing kids how to do science experiments and projects online. She even teamed up with the TV station PBS (Public Broadcasting Service). Her YouTube channel is FullTimeKid.

## Briena and Britney

Briena and Britney are the BOW Girls. They teach kids how to bake and cook. They started making videos in 2013. They've been busy in the kitchen ever since.

## Robby Novak

Robby Novak is called Kid President. At the age of nine, he began starring in inspiring videos. His positive attitude has earned him millions of fans.

Robby's speeches encourage others to try their hardest and be the best they can be.

# Cool Gamers

## Karina Calor

Do you like gaming? Karina Calor sure does. She is known on YouTube as GamerGirl. Karina shows how to play and win the games kids love, like Minecraft.

## Ethan

Ethan is another famous kid gamer. His channel is EthanGamer. Ethan's many fans watch and learn from his quick gaming moves. Some of them have been following him since his first video in 2013.

Online stars connect with gamers all around the world to show them gaming tips and tricks.

# Famous Reviewers

Some online stars have strong opinions. They share what they like and dislike about things.

## Ryan

Ryan loves toys. So he became a toy reviewer. His famous YouTube channel is Ryan ToysReview. It has almost twenty million subscribers.

Ryan has turned reviewing toys into a full-time job.

## Brooke

Brooke began reviewing books online in 2014. She's posted more than two hundred videos to her channel, Studio B. She also makes funny videos about her life.

All of these cool stars are taking charge online. They have fun doing what they love. And their fans love watching them do it!

# You Can Do It!

Do you want to shine online? Talk to a parent or guardian first. Ask if it's OK to make and post videos. If you get a yes, then think of a good idea. Maybe you want to perform skits, review books, or be silly. Make a plan for your video. Next, grab a phone or camera and start filming. You might ask a friend or family member to help.

# Did You Know?

- The Kid President met a real president, Barack Obama. Robby Novak made a video of this famous meeting.
- In 2018, Ryan ToysReview earned more money than any other channel on YouTube.
- YouTube began in 2005 with a small number of users. More than thirty million people use YouTube every day. More than five billion videos have been posted.

# Glossary

**channel:** a web page on YouTube where someone shares videos

**creative:** having an ability to make new things or think of new ideas

**fan:** someone who likes a famous person and watches what that person does

**popular:** something or someone that many people like

**reviewer:** someone who shares opinions about something

**subscriber:** someone who signs up to follow a person's videos on YouTube

**YouTube:** a website where people can post, watch, and share videos

# Further Reading

Grabham, Tim. *Video Ideas*. New York: DK, 2018.

How to Make a Video! Film & Edit Tips for Kids!
https://www.youtube.com/watch?time_continue=2&v=Jk4sqPDHGRE

How to Start a Successful YouTube Channel for Kids!
https://www.youtube.com/watch?v=F81Cjy6oNBk

Kid President
http://kidpresident.com

Owings, Lisa. *YouTube*. Minneapolis: Checkerboard Library, 2017.

YouTube Channel Ideas for Kids! (Ideas for Starting a YouTube Channel for Kids)
https://www.youtube.com/watch?v=dUg-3_hGvkk

Waxman, Laura Hamilton. *Cool Kid Musicians*. Minneapolis: Lerner Publications, 2020.

# Index



# Photo Acknowledgments

Image credits: FatCamera/Getty Images, p. 2; Paul Bradbury/Caiaimage/Getty Images, p. 4; Sharaf Maksumov/Shutterstock.com, p. 5; mimagephotography/Shutterstock.com, p. 6; Spencer Grant/Getty Images, p. 7; Elizabethsalleebauer/Getty Images, p. 8; Hannamariah/Shutterstock.com, p. 9; GagliardiPhotography/Shutterstock.com, p. 10; Steve Debenport/E+/Getty Images, p. 11; Westend61/Getty Images, p. 12; C Flanigan/FilmMagic/Getty Images, p. 13; OHishiapply/Shutterstock.com, p. 14; Miguel Sanz/Getty Images, p. 15; Wealan Pollard/Getty Images, p. 16; ivanastar/Getty Images, p. 17; urbanbuzz/Shutterstock.com, p. 18; gradyreese/Getty Images, p. 19; real444/Getty Images, p. 20; Juj Winn/Moment/Getty Images, p. 22.

Cover: White House Photo by Pete Souza/Alamy Stock Photo.

Main body text set in Billy Infant regular. Typeface provided by SparkType.